GW01464004

I SPY
Music
Instruments

ARE YOU READY?

I SPY with my little eye, something beginning with...

A is for
Acoustic Guitar

I SPY with my little eye, something beginning with...

B

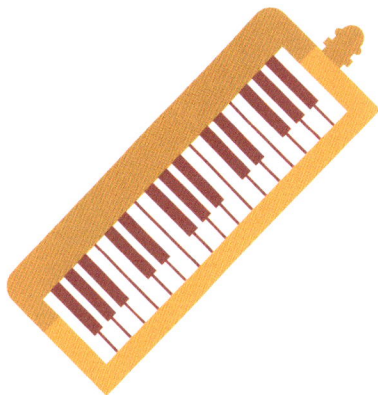

B is for Bugle

I SPY with my little eye, something beginning with...

C is for
Cello

I SPY with my little eye,
something beginning with...

D is for Drums

I SPY with my little eye, something beginning with...

E is for

Erxian

I SPY with my little eye,
something beginning with...

F is for Flute

I SPY with my little eye,
something beginning with...

G
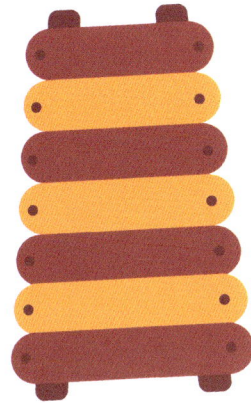

G is for Glockenspiel

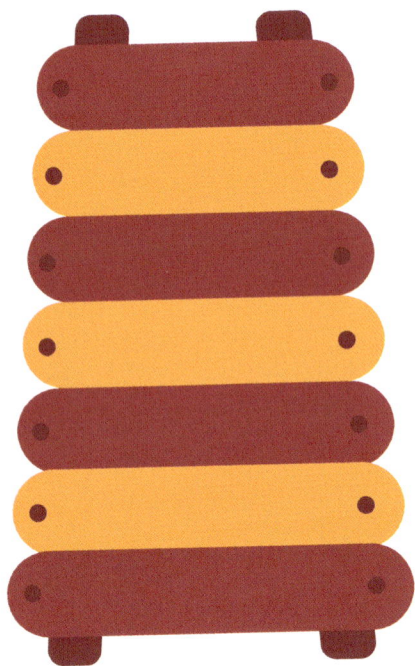

I SPY with my little eye, something beginning with...

H is for Harminica

I SPY with my little eye, something beginning with...

I is for Igil

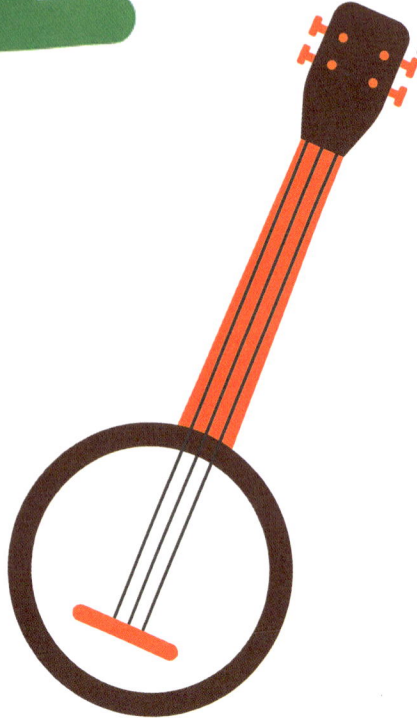

I SPY with my little eye, something beginning with...

J is for Jew's Harp

I SPY with my little eye,
something beginning with...

K

K is for Keyboard

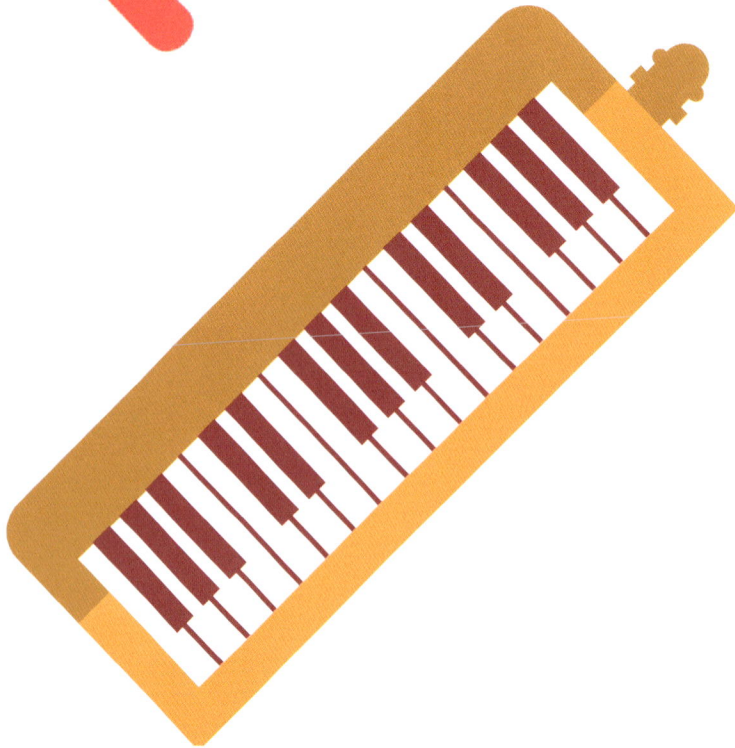

I SPY with my little eye,
something beginning with...

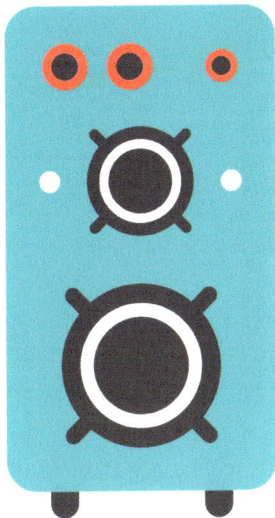

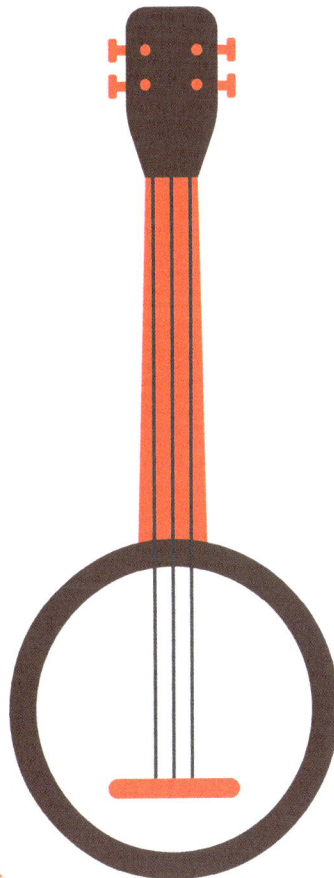

L is for
Lute

I SPY with my little eye, something beginning with...

M

M is for Mandolin

I SPY with my little eye, something beginning with...

O N

N is for Naqara

I SPY with my little eye, something beginning with...

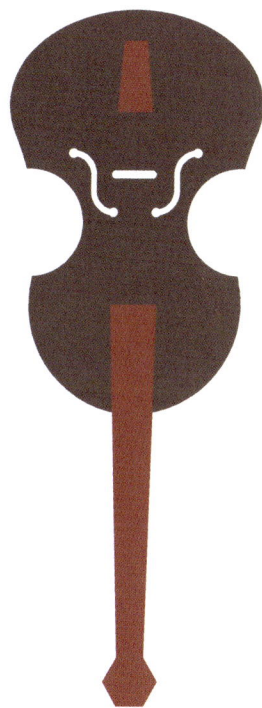

 is for
Organ

I SPY with my little eye, something beginning with...

P is for Planet and moon

I SPY with my little eye, something beginning with...

R is for Recorder

I SPY with my little eye, something beginning with...

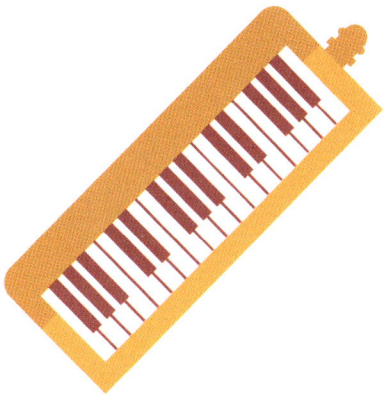

S is for Saxophone

I SPY with my little eye, something beginning with...

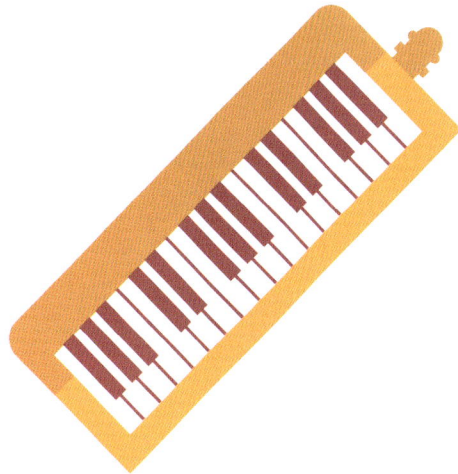

T is for Tamburine

I SPY with my little eye, something beginning with...

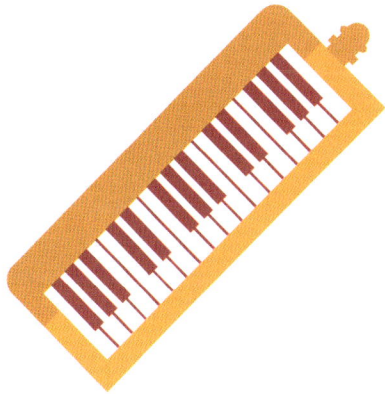

U is for
Ukulele

I SPY with my little eye, something beginning with...

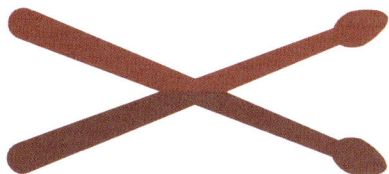

W is for Willow flute

I SPY with my little eye, something beginning with...

Z is for Zhongdihu

Thank You for buying this book. I hope you liked the product. If you can, leave your feedback because it helps me develop a lot. You can also see my other products – Have Fun!

Designed by
Creative Fabrica
Vecteezy

Printed in Great Britain
by Amazon

66615017R00028